100 facts

Animal Life

Barbara Taylor

Consultant: Steve Parker

First published in 2012 by Miles Kelly Publishing Ltd
Harding's Barn, Bardfield End Green, Thaxted, Essex, CM6 3PX, UK

Copyright © Miles Kelly Publishing Ltd 2012

10 9 8 7 6 5 4 3 2 1

Publishing Director Belinda Gallagher
Creative Director Jo Cowan
Editorial Director Rosie McGuire
Editor Sarah Parkin
Volume Designer Andrea Slane
Cover Designer Kayleigh Allen
Image Manager Liberty Newton
Indexer Jane Parker
Production Manager Elizabeth Collins
Reprographics Stephan Davis,
Anthony Cambray, Jennifer Hunt,
Thom Allaway

ISBN 978-1-84810-562-1

Printed in China

British Library Cataloguing-in-Publication Data
A catalogue record for this book is available from the British Library

ACKNOWLEDGEMENTS

The publishers would like to thank the following artists who have
contributed to this book:

Julian Baker, Mike Foster, Stuart Jackson-Carter, Mike Saunders

All other artwork from the Miles Kelly Artwork Bank

The publishers would like to thank the following sources for the use of
their photographs:

t = top, b = bottom, l = left, r = right, c = centre, bg = background

Cover Front: Mark Bridger/Shutterstock, Back: Digital Stock

Alamy 22(bl) Antje Schulte – Spiders and Co.; 38(tr) Aditya "Dicky" Singh

Dreamstime.com 6(fish) Goodolga

FLPA 14–15 Elliott Neep; 18(c) Chris Stenger/Minden Pictures;
19(t) ImageBroker/Imagebroker; 20(r) Piotr Naskrecki/Minden Pictures;
21(br) Paul Sawer; 23(b) Mitsuaki Iwago/Minden Pictures; 25(b) Claus
Meyer/Minden Pictures; 31(b) ImageBroker/Imagebroker; 33(t) Robin
Chittenden; 36 Suzi Eszterhas/Minden Pictures, (bl) Frans Lanting;
37(tr) Yva Momatiuk & John Eastcott/Minden Pictures; 38(c) Pete
Oxford/Minden Pictures, (b) Gerry Ellis/Minden Pictures; 39(t) Colin
Marshall, (b) Thomas Marent/Minden Pictures

Fotolia.com 2 pdtnc; 6(reptile) Paul Murphy

iStockphoto.com 8(bg) Miguel Angelo Silva

Naturepl.com 8(c) Brandon Cole; 13(b) Brandon Cole; 17(b) Nature
Production; 24 Jurgen Freund; 25(r) Anup Shah; 34–35 Fred Olivier;
35(r) Shattil & Rozinski

Photoshot 15(l) Woodfall; 30–31 NHPA

Shutterstock.com 1 Dhoxax; 3(b) Trevor Kelly; 4–5 Igor Janicek;
6(invertebrate) Richard Waters, (amphibian) Audrey Snider-Bell,
(bird) Steve Byland; 7(t) Thomas Barrat, (b) Rita Januskeviciute;
9(t) FloridaStock, (b) gillmar; 10(t) Pan Xunbin, (b) wim claes; 11(t) Ivan
Kuzmin; 12(paper and notebook) nuttakit; 15(br) Cathy Keifer;
16(t) Geoffrey Kuchera, (c) Audrey Snider-Bell, (bl) Dirk Ercken;
18–19 Anna Omelchenko; 19(c) Steven Russell Smith Photos; 23(r) Norma
Cornes; 24(t) Eric Gevaert; 26(bl) Nancy Kennedy; 27(r) Neale Cousland;
28–29 Krzysztof Odziomek; 29(b) Specta; 30(tl) EcoPrint;
32 worldswildlifewonders; 34(c) Ecostock; 35(tl) Wayne Duguay;
38–39(bg) House @ Brasil Art Studio; 38(paper and tape) sharpner;
39(c) Janelle Lugge

All other photographs are from:
Corel, Digital Stock, digitalvision, ImageState, John Foxx, PhotoAlto,
PhotoDisc, PhotoEssentials, PhotoPro, Stockbyte

Every effort has been made to acknowledge
the source and copyright holder of each picture.
Miles Kelly Publishing apologises for any
unintentional errors or omissions.

Made with paper from a sustainable forest

www.mileskelly.net
info@mileskelly.net
www.factsforprojects.com

CONTENTS

Animal planet

Our planet is full of animals. They live almost everywhere, from the tops of mountains to the darkest depths of oceans. The greatest variety of animals live in places such as rainforests or coral reefs, where there is plenty of food and shelter.

▼ African animals gather round a waterhole in the dry season. The great grasslands of Africa are one of the last places where huge herds of grazing animals still survive.

2 Animals come in all shapes and sizes. Some, such as elephants, are giants, while others, such as fleas, are almost too small to see. There are at least five million different kinds of animals alive today. Scientists discover new kinds every day.

3 For at least 650 million years, animals have been living on our planet. Sponges are among the oldest known animals. They live in oceans today, but remains of sponges that lived 650 million years ago have been found preserved in Australia.

What is an animal?

4 Animals are living things that need to eat food, such as plants or other animals. This gives them the energy they need to survive. Animals use their senses to detect food and react to their surroundings.

▶ Animals can be divided into groups according to their features. Each group has certain characteristics in common.

5 An animal's body is usually made of many cells, which are grouped into tissues. Tissues may be joined together to form organs, such as the brain, heart or lungs, which have different jobs to do.

▼ The organs inside a chimpanzee are very similar to those inside a human being.

Lungs for breathing

Kidneys to process wastes

Intestines to digest food

Brain (inside skull) to control the body

Heart to pump blood around the body

Animal families

Invertebrates are usually small creatures, such as crabs and insects. Some have a hard shell, others are soft.

Fish live in the waters of oceans, rivers and lakes. They breathe in oxygen from the water through flaps called gills.

Amphibians, such as frogs, live partly in water and partly on land. Most lay eggs in water.

Reptiles, such as snakes and lizards, usually live on land in warm places. Most baby reptiles hatch out of eggs.

Birds have wings instead of arms, and most can fly. All birds lay eggs that have a hard shell.

Mammals, such as bears, dolphins and humans, are covered in fur or hair. They breathe air, even if they live in water.

6 Well over 90 percent of all animals are invertebrates. These animals do not have an internal backbone to support their bodies. They rely on the support of their body fluids or a hard outer casing, called an exoskeleton.

7 Animals with a backbone are called vertebrates. Their backbone forms part of an internal skeleton, which is usually made of bone. However, sharks and rays have a skeleton made of rubbery cartilage. A skeleton supports the body, helps it to move and protects the internal organs.

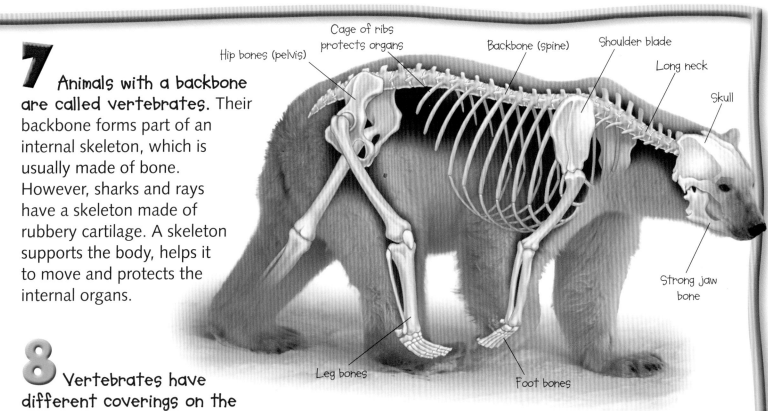

Hip bones (pelvis)

Cage of ribs protects organs

Backbone (spine)

Shoulder blade

Long neck

Skull

Strong jaw bone

Leg bones

Foot bones

8 Vertebrates have different coverings on the outsides of their bodies. Fish and reptiles have scales made from hard skin or bone. Frogs usually have smooth skin. Birds are the only animals with feathers, and mammals are the only animals with fur or hair.

▲ A polar bear has a short, strong backbone and powerful leg and hip bones. Its skull is long and slim to help it swim.

▶ Foals will feed from their mothers for several months, or up to one year in the wild.

9 Humans are mammals. Mammals are the most intelligent of all animals. Female mammals feed their young on milk, which they produce themselves. There are about 5500 different kinds of mammals and up to one-quarter of them are bats!

On the move

10 Most animals move around to find food, water or shelter, or escape from danger. Many use muscles to pull their skeleton into different positions. Others are carried along by wind or water currents.

▶ The powerful swimming muscles of the striped marlin make it one of the fastest fish in the ocean. It can swim at speeds of up to 80 kilometres an hour.

Streamlined snout

12 Eels are long fish that swim by wriggling their bodies from side to side. Penguins and turtles use flippers to propel themselves through the water. Most fish use their tails to move forwards and their fins to steer, balance or slow down.

11 Some invertebrates, such as corals or sponges, spend all (or part) of their lives in one place. These are called sessile animals and they usually live in water.

Dorsal fin

Swim bladder helps marlin to float

Tail

Muscles

Pectoral fin

13 Squid and octopuses move around by jet propulsion. They draw water into an internal chamber called a mantle cavity. Then they force the water out of their body through a narrow, bendy funnel called a siphon.

▼ Scallops swim by opening and closing the two halves of their shell. This forces water out between the halves and pushes them through the water.

① The shell is open

② The shell claps shut and water shoots out in a backwards jet

③ The shell opens again and water is sucked back inside

▼ An eagle's powerful chest muscles are joined to a large, flat part of its breastbone called the keel. These muscles pull its huge wings up and down as it soars through the sky.

Arm bones

Tail feathers

Wing feathers

Keel

Chest muscles

Wing covers (elytra)

14 Birds, insects and bats are the only animals capable of powered flight. They have lightweight bodies and powerful muscles to flap their wings. A bird's wings are arm bones covered in feathers. A bat's wings are made of skin stretched between finger bones.

Flying wings

◄ A ladybird protects its delicate flying wings under two wing covers, called elytra.

15 Most amphibians, reptiles and some mammals walk with their feet flat on the ground. Some animals, such as ostriches, cats and dogs, walk and run on their toes, allowing them to move more quickly. A horse's hooves are at the tips of its toes.

I DON'T BELIEVE IT!

The peregrine falcon is the fastest animal in the world. It dives down to catch its prey at speeds of up to 322 kilometres an hour!

► Strong claws help wolves to grip slippery ground so they can cover long distances quickly.

Super senses

16 Animals sense the world around them through seeing, hearing, smelling, touching and tasting. An animal's senses also supply information about its own body, such as whether it is too hot or too cold.

Sight

▶ A fly's huge compound eyes are good at picking up movement over a wide area. The fly's brain puts together the images from all the eye units to create a complete picture.

Hearing

Ears move backwards and forwards to detect danger

17 Many animals have eyes to detect light. Insects have compound eyes made up of hundreds of tiny eyes with one or more lenses. Animals with bigger eyes may have a slit in the middle of the eye called a pupil, which controls the amount of light entering the eye.

18 Mammals are the only animals with ear flaps that funnel sounds into the ear. The sounds hit an eardrum, which vibrates. Tiny bones pass on the vibrations to a fluid-filled chamber in the inner ear. Receptors in the inner ear send signals to the mammal's brain, which 'hears' the sound.

◀ A rabbit's big ears can be turned in different directions to locate the source of a sound, or even listen to two sounds at the same time.

19 An animal's senses of taste and smell often work together. A snake flicks its forked tongue in and out of its mouth to smell and taste the air. Most vertebrates taste with their tongues, but adult insects often taste with their feet!

▶ Snakes have special smell detectors on the roofs of their mouths, so they use their tongues to pick up smells in the air.

TRUE OR FALSE?

1. Insects have sensory feelers called tentacles.
2. The pupil controls the amount of light entering the eye.
3. Birds are the only animals with ear flaps.

Answers:
1. False. The feelers are called antennae. 2. True. 3. False. Mammals are the only animals with ear flaps

20 Many animals, such as insects and crabs, have two long, thin feelers called antennae on their heads. The antennae help to detect and identify smells, air currents and textures. Male moths often have feathery antennae to pick up the scent given off by female moths.

21 A sense of touch provides information about an animal's immediate surroundings and the position of its body. Most animals have touch receptors all over their bodies. Some receptors are linked to structures such as whiskers.

Whiskers

▼ The star-nosed mole is named after the sensitive tentacles around its nose, which help it to find prey in dark, underground tunnels. Its nose is six times more sensitive to touch than the human hand.

Touch

Food and eating

22 Animals eat a range of food, including plants, other animals and dead remains. Some have a varied diet. Others eat a narrow range of food – koalas eat mainly eucalyptus leaves.

23 There are three main groups animals can be divided into. Plant-eaters are called herbivores, meat-eaters are called carnivores and animals that eat plants and meat are called omnivores. Food chains show how animals are linked together by what they eat.

FOOD CHAIN

Fox

Mouse

Grasshopper

Grass

◀ Food chains link animals together according to what they eat. Food chains always start with plants, because they can make their own food using the Sun's energy.

FOOD WEB

Fox

Owl

Mouse

Snake

Grasshopper

Frog

Rabbit

Grass

▲ Animals are usually part of several different food chains. This means that two or more food chains can be linked together into a network called a food web.

24 Food is easier to digest in small pieces. Many animals have teeth to tear, chew or grind up their food. Some animals without teeth, such as spiders and scorpions, inject digestive juices into their food and then suck up the 'soup' this produces.

▶ Carnivores have pointed teeth to seize and tear prey, and sharp cheek teeth to slice up meat or crack bones. Herbivores have lots of grinding teeth to mash up tough plants.

Carnivore (fox)   Herbivore (camel)

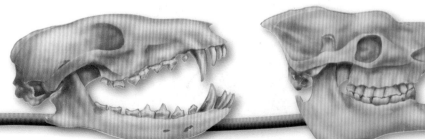

▶ The shape of a bird's bill is suited to its diet and where it finds food.

Toucans use their long bills to reach fruit

Puffins carry small fish in their bills

Coal tits probe for insects with their thin, pointed bills

25 Birds have a lightweight, toothless bill instead of a heavy jaw bone and teeth. The shape and size of a bird's bill depends on the kind of food it eats. Birds swallow their food whole and grind it up in a muscular part of their stomach, called the gizzard.

26 Filter-feeders collect tiny particles of food from the water. They use special body parts that work like sieves to trap the food. These include the baleen plates of some whales, the fringed bills of flamingos and the feathery gills of peacock worms.

▶ Humpback whales strain fish and plankton from the water using fringed plates of baleen in their gigantic jaws.

MAKE A FOOD CHAIN

You will need:
pencil   paper   coloured pens   scissors   tape   ribbon

Draw and colour a picture of a plant, a herbivore and a carnivore. Cut them out. Stick each of your pictures to a length of ribbon, with the carnivore at the top and the plant at the bottom, to make your food chain.

Predators and prey

27 An animal that hunts and eats other animals is called a predator. Its victim is known as its prey. Predators have to find, catch and kill their prey. They need strength, keen senses, quick reactions and lethal weapons.

28 After dark, many predators rely on their excellent sense of hearing to find prey. Some bats hunt insects at night by producing high-pitched squeaks. They listen for the echoes that bounce back from their prey.

▼ Bats have large ears to pick up the sound echoes bouncing back from their prey.

Sounds made by bat

Echoes from prey

29 Some predators hide and wait for their prey to come to them. They may build traps, such as the webs of spiders, or lure their prey within close reach. The alligator snapping turtle has a false 'worm' on its tongue to make fish swim right into its open jaws.

'Worm'

◄ The alligator snapping turtle wriggles the 'worm' on its tongue to make it look alive. It stabs larger prey with the hooked tips of its strong jaws.

◀ ▶ A cheetah can only run at top speed for a few hundred metres before it gets too hot and exhausted, and has to stop. If this warthog keeps running, it might get away.

30 Active predators need a set of weapons for attacking and killing their prey without being injured themselves. These weapons range from pointed teeth and powerful jaws, to curved claws, sharp bills and poisonous stings or fangs.

◀ Ospreys use their strong, needle-sharp claws, called talons, to snatch fish from the water. Spines under their toes help them to hold their slippery prey.

31 Many spiders are agile, fast-moving hunters that stalk their prey. Jumping spiders prowl around, using their eight eyes to spot a meal. They pounce on their prey and kill it with a bite from their poisonous fangs.

▶ Chameleons creep very slowly along branches, but they shoot out their long, sticky tongues at lightning speed to catch insects.

32 Some predators save energy by sneaking up on their prey, then attacking suddenly at the last minute. Many are well camouflaged (see page 16) so they can creep close to their prey.

Survival skills

33 The world is a dangerous place for animals, and they have different ways of staying alive. Many move fast to escape an attack. Others are protected by armour-plating, thick shells, horns, tusks or spines.

34 Animals may have colours, patterns or shapes that help them to blend in with their surroundings. Some disguise themselves by looking like twigs, thorns or leaves. This is called camouflage.

▼ A poison arrow frog makes poison in its skin. Just a few drops of this poison are strong enough to kill an animal as big as a horse.

▲ A rattlesnake shakes the 'rattle' on its tail to warn predators to keep away.

35 Brightly coloured animals are often poisonous. Their colours are a warning message, which means "I am dangerous, don't eat me!" Predators learn to leave these animals alone. Harmless animals may copy these warning colours to protect themselves. This is known as mimicry.

Bony plates covered by horny keratin

36 Slow-moving animals often rely on body armour for protection. Tortoises and turtles can pull their soft body parts inside their shells. Armadillos, pangolins and pill millipedes roll up into a ball to protect their soft undersides.

① Armadillo curls into a ball if it senses danger

▲ A three-banded armadillo has body armour on its back, but not underneath. When it rolls up into a tight ball, its body armour protects its soft underparts.

Underside of body is soft and hairy

② Armadillo starts to uncurl when it is safe again

Flexible skin between bands of armour

37 Predators prefer to eat living prey, so some animals survive an attack by pretending to be dead. Snakes such as the grass snake are good at playing dead. They roll onto their backs, open their mouths and keep still. The snake starts to move again when the predator goes away.

③ Armadillo is protected by body armour even when walking

38 Some animals can break off parts of their bodies to escape from predators. Lizards may break off a tail tip, which wriggles about on the ground. This distracts an attacker, giving the lizard time to escape.

▲ The bright blue tail of this skink, a type of lizard, breaks at special fracture points between the bones inside the tail.

Living in groups

39 Many animals, including some insects, fish, birds and mammals, live in groups with others of their kind. They are called social animals and may have female or male leaders.

▼ Cape fur seals gather on shorelines in colonies of up to 270,000 individuals to breed and look after their pups.

40 Other animals, such as bears, tigers and orang-utans, live on their own. They do not have to share their food and are able to have young if they find a mate. In a group of social animals, such as wolves, only one pair of animals may have babies.

41 Some animals live in groups just for the breeding season. Penguins and seals form large breeding colonies with hundreds, or even thousands, of members. They warn each other of nearby predators and parents may leave their young in 'nurseries' when they go to find food.

▲ Flamingos live in colonies that may contain thousands of birds. This helps them to avoid predators and find food.

▲ Male lions (far right) are bigger than females. Their thick manes of hair make them look even bigger and more frightening to their enemies.

42 **Lions are one of the few social cats.** They live in groups called prides, which consist of several related lionesses, their cubs, and one or more adult males. The males protect the pride from predators and rival lions, while the females do most of the hunting.

43 **The young of most insects have to fend for themselves.** However, ants and termites, some types of bees and a few wasps live in giant family groups. One or more females lay eggs, while other members of the group care for the young and defend the nest.

▶ Honeybees form a tightly-packed ball of bees, called a swarm, when they leave their nest to start a new colony.

Signals and signs

44 Animals give each other information by means of a variety of signals and signs. This is called communication. It usually involves giving a warning, telling each other where food is or attracting a mate.

▶ Meerkats take turns to watch for predators. They give a sharp bark or a whistle to warn members of their group.

45 Many animals show off colourful body parts to find a mate. To impress females, male frigate birds puff out their bright red throat sacs, and male anole lizards flash their colourful throat flaps. Other visual signals that attract mates include the flashing lights of fireflies.

▼ Howler monkeys have a special voice box and throat pouch that make their calls loud. Males have louder, deeper calls than females and can be heard up to 5 kilometres away.

◀ Blue-footed boobies lift and spread their bright blue feet to impress their partners.

46 Sound signals are often used by a group of animals to tell others of their kind to keep out of their area, or territory. Howler monkeys claim their territories in thick rainforests using loud calls. Even though they can't see each other, the calls can still be heard.

47 When animals live in groups, body language is often the best way to communicate. This is less likely to attract the attention of a predator than loud sounds or bright colours. A chimp's facial expressions signal its mood.

Worried face

Excited face

Play face

▲ With their big eyes and flexible lips, chimps are good at pulling faces to communicate with each other. They also use at least 66 different gestures to 'talk' to each other.

48 The long, striped tails of ring-tailed lemurs help them to keep in touch with other members of their group. Males spread scent from their arms over their tails and wave them at rival lemur groups in 'stink battles' to defend their territory.

49 Some forms of communication involve combinations of sounds, smells and movement, which are called displays. During the breeding season, male deer roar, spread scent and fight each other with their antlers to win a group of females for mating.

▼ Male fallow deer lock antlers and try to push each other backwards. A pair will only fight if they are evenly matched in size and strength.

Eggs and babies

50 All animals can make new life like themselves – this is called reproduction. Some animals can reproduce without mating. Sea anemones reproduce by splitting into two.

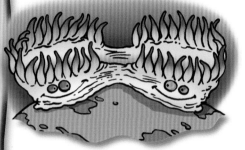

▶ Baby seahorses develop inside a pouch on the front of the male's body. The babies hatch out when they are between two and seven weeks old. They swim out of the pouch and fend for themselves straight away.

51 Many animals mate to produce fertilized eggs. The eggs may develop outside the female's body or stay inside her until they are born. In some animals, such as tigers, pairs of males and females stay together only for mating, but in others, such as swans, they remain together for life.

52 Most fish, amphibians, reptiles, insects, spiders and birds lay eggs. A few unusual mammals, such as the platypus, also lay eggs. Eggs can be many different shapes, sizes and textures. They may be small and soft, like fish eggs, or larger, with a hard shell, like birds' eggs.

Egg cocoon

◀ Spiders, such as this wasp spider, protect their eggs by spinning a cocoon of silk around them.

Yolk sac contains food

Developing chick

Egg white supplies proteins, water and vitamins

Strong shell has pores (tiny holes) to allow air to pass through

Egg tooth

▲ The egg holds and protects the bird as it develops. The baby bird breaks out of the shell using its pointed egg tooth.

53 Birds lay eggs because they would be too heavy to fly if they carried their young inside them. A bird's egg contains the developing bird, along with a store of food and a supply of air.

54 Most baby mammals grow inside their mother in a sac called the womb. They feed and breathe through an organ called the placenta. The length of time a baby stays in the womb varies from only 25 days for rats to nearly two years for elephants.

55 Pouched mammals, such as kangaroos, give birth to very small, poorly developed young. The baby crawls into its mother's pouch, where it feeds on her milk until it is fully developed. A baby kangaroo stays in the pouch for about six months.

Bladder

Womb (uterus)

Placenta

Cord links baby to placenta

Birth canal

▲ A baby elephant develops inside a protective sac of liquid inside its mother's womb.

◄ A tiny red kangaroo feeds from a teat inside its mother's pouch.

Growing up

56 A series of changes take place during an animal's life — it grows, produces young and dies. This is called a life cycle. The life cycle of some insects lasts for only a few weeks, but the life cycle of a giant tortoise may last over 100 years.

▲ A mother tiger carries her cubs by the loose skin at the scruff of the neck to move them to a safe place.

▲ Under the cover of darkness, baby turtles race down to the sea as soon as they hatch out of their eggs on the beach. Many are caught by predators.

57 Animals that produce lots of young, such as fish, do not usually look after them. The large numbers mean that some of the young will manage to survive. Animals with fewer babies, such as mammals, almost all birds and some reptiles, often feed and protect their young during early life.

58 Some animals, such as bear cubs and baby owls, are helpless when they are born. Others, such as zebras, deer and ducklings, can run around soon after birth. This helps them to escape from predators and keep up with other members of their group.

59 Some young animals, such as tadpoles and caterpillars, look very different from their parents. They change their body shape as they mature into adults. Tadpoles change into frogs and caterpillars change into butterflies.

① Egg

② Caterpillar

▲ Butterflies have four stages in their life cycle. The pupa goes through a dramatic change called metamorphosis as it changes into an adult butterfly.

③ Pupa

④ Adult butterfly

▼ A baby giraffe, or calf, can stand up and walk about one hour after it is born. When the calf grows bigger, its mother will leave it with other young giraffes in a 'nursery' with an adult 'babysitter'.

60 Animals with a hard outer body casing, such as insects, spiders and crabs, have to shed their body casing in order to grow. This is called moulting. The soft skin underneath quickly expands and hardens to form a new, bigger casing.

61 Baby animals grow and learn at different rates. Mice are ready to leave the nest when they are only two or three weeks old, while orang-utans, gorillas, tigers and elephants spend many years raising their young.

◀ Some birds have chicks that are blind when they hatch. Their parents feed them and they grow fast.

Animal homes

62 Homes shelter animals from the weather and help to protect them from predators. They may also be used to store food and raise young. Some animals build a new home every year, others stay in their old one, making it larger and more secure.

◄ Weaver bird nests often hang from the ends of branches to make it harder for predators to reach them.

63 Most birds build nests to keep their eggs and babies warm, and hide them from danger. They use a wide range of nesting materials from twigs, grass and moss, to feathers, mud and pebbles. Male weaver birds loop, knot and twist grass together to make complex nests.

64 Some animals, such as tortoises and snails, carry their homes around with them as a shell on their backs. The shell is part of the animal's body, and it can pull its body inside the shell to avoid predators or bad weather.

▼ Rabbits live in a maze of underground tunnels and chambers called a warren.

▼ A hermit crab lives inside an empty shell to protect the soft rear part of its body. Its borrowed home once contained the body of a shellfish, such as a whelk.

65 Termites build huge mounds of rock-hard soil above their nest, which is home to millions of termites. Inside their nest are stores of food, nurseries for the eggs and young, and a chamber for the queen, who lays all the eggs. Chimneys inside the mound let hot air escape and keep the nest cool.

▶ Termite towers as large as this one may take ten, or even as long as 50 years to build! These mud skyscrapers help the tiny termites to survive in hot, dry places.

66 Many small mammals and a few birds live in narrow tunnels underground, where predators find it hard to follow them. These animals use their strong claws for digging. Their tunnels include lots of entrances and exits, so they can escape easily.

Living in water

▼ Dolphins have to come to the water's surface to breathe air through a blowhole on the top of their heads. Their streamlined shape helps them to swim fast.

67 The water of oceans, rivers, lakes and swamps supports an animal's body. Many animal giants, such as whales, live in the oceans for this reason. Watery habitats are good places for animals to live because they contain plenty of food and places to shelter.

68 Some animals, such as crocodiles, surface to breathe in oxygen from the air. Others, such as fish, absorb oxygen directly from the water into their blood through thin flaps, called gills.

▲ A basking shark swims along with its huge mouth wide open. Tiny floating creatures are trapped on bristles in front of the gills.

69 Water animals usually have a smooth, streamlined shape and a slippery body that slides through water easily. Many, such as frogs, otters and hippos, have webs of skin between their toes to help them swim. Leeches have suckers to cling onto rocks in fast-flowing rivers.

Webbed feet

◀ An otter's long, flexible body and webbed feet give it power and manoeuvrability in the water. Its strong, thick tail helps it to steer.

70 Most deep-sea animals have watery flesh to help them resist the crushing water pressures. Prey is scarce, so predators have huge mouths and stomachs to eat as much as possible whenever they find a meal.

▼ The huge, pointed teeth of the fangtooth grab and hold other fish in the deep sea. Its teeth are no good for chewing, so the fangtooth swallows its prey whole.

71 On shorelines, shellfish, such as whelks, have thick shells to withstand pounding waves. At low tide on sandy or muddy shores, worms and crabs burrow underground so their bodies will not dry out.

▼ A coral reef is made from the skeletons of dead corals, which are tiny animals related to sea anemones. Living corals perch on top and use their stinging tentacles to catch food.

72 Coral reef animals often have bright colours and patterns, which may help them to recognize others of their kind. Colours may also help to attract a mate or provide camouflage for both predators, such as coral groupers, and prey, such as weedy sea dragons.

Desert survivors

73 The greatest challenge to animals in deserts is the lack of water. Scorpions and reptiles have watertight body coverings, which lose little water. Kangaroo rats get all the water they need from their food.

◀ Scorpions can survive without water for several months.

74 To avoid the daytime heat, many desert animals sleep in underground burrows or inside cacti. They come out when the temperature drops at night. Some animals use their bodies to stay cool. The giant ears of the fennec fox give off heat, and the ground squirrel uses its tail as a sunshade.

75 Feathers are good at keeping heat out, which stops birds overheating in the day. They are also good at keeping birds warm during the bitterly cold desert nights and winters. The poor-will avoids the desert winter altogether by going into a deep sleep, called hibernation.

◀ The fennec fox's huge ears help it to hear its small prey. Hairs inside the ears help to keep out the dust and sand of the desert.

QUIZ

1. What does a camel store inside its humps?
2. Why does a fennec fox have big ears?
3. How long can a scorpion last without water?

Answers:
1. Fat 2. To give off heat and to hear its small prey 3. Several months

▶ The darkling beetle of the Namib Desert holds its abdomen high in the air to catch moisture, which runs down into its mouth.

Long legs lift body above hot sand

76 Moving over hot ground or shifting sands can be difficult. Camels and addax (a type of antelope) have wide, tough footpads to stop their feet burning or sinking into the sand.

▲ Sidewinder snakes avoid the hot sand by flinging their bodies through the air in a series of sideways leaps. They hardly touch the hot sand.

77 Most mammals have fat under their skin all over their bodies, but this stops them cooling down. Camels store all their fat in their humps, so the rest of their body loses heat quickly. Bactrian camels have thick fur to keep them warm in the cold winters of the Gobi Desert.

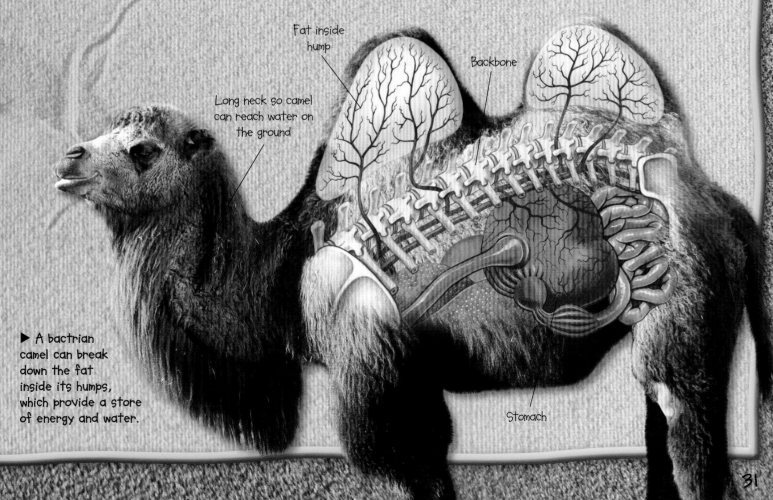

Fat inside hump

Backbone

Long neck so camel can reach water on the ground

Stomach

▶ A bactrian camel can break down the fat inside its humps, which provide a store of energy and water.

Life in the trees

78 Rainforests make good habitats (places to live) because they are warm and wet all year round. However, animals living there have to compete for living space and avoid the many predators. In temperate forests, animals have to cope with cold winters.

▼ Wallace's flying frog spreads its webbed feet to slow down its fall as it jumps from tree to tree.

79 Forest animals are good at climbing, swinging and gliding through the trees. Gibbons have long arms to swing from branch to branch, while some monkeys and snakes have special prehensile (gripping) tails. Some animals, such as flying frogs or sugar gliders, glide from tree to tree on flaps of thin skin.

80 Predators lurk at all levels of the rainforests. There are fierce birds of prey such as hawks and eagles in the canopy (treetops). Snakes and woodpeckers make their homes in the branches. The forest floor is inhabited by tigers, bears and spiders.

▼ A spider monkey has a strong prehensile tail, which allows it to hang from branches.

▶ This white-necked Jacobin hummingbird builds its shallow nest of plants and cobwebs on top of a wide leaf. It lives in the forests of Central and South America.

82 Forests provide a good choice of nesting places for birds. Parrots, toucans and owls nest inside tree holes. Many birds nest high in the trees to keep their eggs and young out of reach of most predators.

81 Many forest animals are nocturnal (come out at night). Their senses are specially adapted to help them thrive in the dark. They may have huge eyes and ears, or extra-sensitive noses. Snakes such as pit vipers can sense the heat given off by birds and mammals and track their prey in total darkness.

▼ The greater musky fruit bat of the Philippines eats the fruit of rainforest trees. It spits out the seeds, which may grow into new trees.

MONKEY MASK

You will need:
colouring paints and pencils
paper plate   paper   scissors
glue   ribbon or string
Paint a paper plate brown. On the paper, draw two eyes, a nose, a mouth and two ears. Cut them out and glue them onto the paper plate. Carefully cut holes in the eyes. Then make holes in the sides of the plate and use ribbon or string to tie the mask to your face.

83 Forest animals are closely linked with plants, helping to spread pollen and seeds. Brightly coloured birds called quetzals spread the seeds of avocado trees. Brazil nut trees rely on guinea pig-like agoutis to break open their tough seed cases with their strong teeth.

Out in the cold

84 Many animals have to survive in the coldest environments on Earth. Land animals living there rely on thick fur or feathers to keep them warm. Small, round ears and muzzles help to reduce heat loss.

85 Some animals live in cold oceans. Walruses and seals rely on a thick layer of fat, called blubber, under their skin to keep them warm. This is because fur and feathers are not so good at trapping heat when they are wet.

86 Animals living in places where it snows in winter sometimes turn white for camouflage. The Arctic fox, snowshoe hare, ptarmigan and stoat all have white coats in winter to help them blend in with their snowy surroundings. When the snow melts, they turn brown or grey to match the summer landscape.

▲ The walrus has a layer of fatty blubber up to 10 centimetres thick. Its flat flippers support its heavy body on land.

▲ The snowy owl's white feathers provide good camouflage as it hunts for small mammals to eat.

88 Some animals, such as ice-fish, survive at temperatures well below freezing. This is because they have a chemical 'anti-freeze' in their blood. The 'anti-freeze' stops ice crystals from forming inside their bodies so they don't freeze solid.

87 Slippery ice, deep snow and steep mountain slopes can make it hard to get around. The long, furry back feet of snowshoe hares stop them sinking into the snow, while polar bears have non-slip soles.

89 High on mountains, the thin air makes it difficult to take in oxygen. Animals such as mountain goats have large lungs to breathe in as much air as possible. They also have more red blood cells to collect oxygen from the air, and bigger hearts to pump blood full of oxygen around their bodies.

▶ Mountain goats have sharp, pointed hooves, with two toes that spread wide to improve their balance. Rough pads on the bottom of each toe provide good grip.

◀ Emperor penguins huddle together for warmth and protection in the freezing Antarctic winters.

Incredible journeys

▶ Thousands of wildebeest swim through rivers on their yearly migration across the African grasslands. They follow the rains in search of fresh grass to eat.

90 Some animals make regular journeys, called migrations, from one place to another. They move to areas suited to breeding, or to avoid overcrowding or cold or dry seasons. Migrations take place on land, in water and in the air.

91 There are birds and whales that migrate thousands of kilometres each year. Monarch butterflies travel 4000 kilometres from Canada every year, to spend the winter in Mexico.

◀ Monarch butterflies rest through the winter in forests of pine trees high in the mountains of Mexico. Butterflies in the middle of a cluster are warmer and safer from bird attacks.

92 Fish such as salmon migrate at different stages in their lives. Adult salmon live in the oceans, where there is more food, but they migrate to rivers to breed. European eels migrate in the opposite direction: adults live in rivers, but they migrate to the Sargasso Sea to breed.

► Vast numbers of sockeye salmon swim from the sea to the rivers where they were born to lay their eggs. Ten million may migrate up one river in a single season.

93 Adult animals may show young ones which way to go on migration journeys. However many, such as eels, rely on instinct to find their way. Animals also navigate using familiar landmarks, sounds, scents, the positions of the Sun, Moon and stars, and the Earth's magnetic field.

▼ Chemical reactions in the eyes of birds may help them to sense the Earth's magnetic field. This could help them to keep flying in the right direction during long migrations.

Earth's magnetic field

Bobolinks use magnetic clues to navigate from South America to North America each year

I DON'T BELIEVE IT!
Caribou make the longest trek of any land mammal. They travel more than 5000 kilometres a year — that's about the distance from New York to London!

94 Lemmings make regular seasonal migrations between summer and winter areas. They also make more erratic journeys every few years when their numbers grow too large for their food supply. These animals set off to look for food on journeys that have no particular destination. Migrations like this are called irruptions.

Endangered animals

95 Endangered animals are in danger of dying out, or becoming extinct, in the near future. Many are threatened by the things people do, such as destroying their habitats or by hunting them.

◄ Some scientists are trying to protect rare tigers by fitting them with radio collars. They can track their movements in the wild and work out the best ways to save them.

96 Many endangered animals, such as Galapagos giant tortoises, live on small islands. They are specially adapted to survive in one small area, and are not good at surviving the rapid changes that happen when people settle on islands.

◄ Giant tortoises stand a better chance of survival now that people are protecting their eggs and babies.

97 There are now only about 1600 giant pandas left in the wild in China, but numbers are slowly increasing. Panda reserves in bamboo forests are being linked together and illegal killing of pandas has been reduced.

▼ Several giant pandas bred in captivity have now been released into the wild.

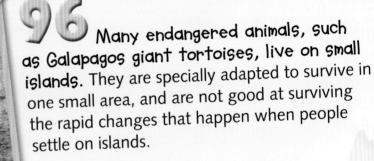

RARE ANIMALS POSTER

You will need:
pen   paper   atlas   glue   pictures of rare animals

Using a pen and paper, trace a world map from an atlas. Write the names of the continents on your map. Stick pictures of rare animals in the places where they live.

98

Rhinos were once widespread in Africa and Asia, but today, most rhinos only survive inside national parks and reserves. They are endangered by habitat loss and illegal trade in rhino horn for traditional Asian medicines.

▲ Over 20,000 southern white rhinos survive in protected sanctuaries. This rhino has a particularly long front horn.

99

Albatrosses usually fish from the surface of the sea. When they see long lines of fishing hooks floating behind fishing boats, they fly down to steal the bait on the hooks. Unfortunately, some birds swallow the hooks, are dragged underwater and drown.

◄ Albatrosses can be saved by different fishing methods, such as sinking the lines deeper underwater.

100

Our closest living relatives are great apes, like us – bonobos, chimps, gorillas and orang-utans. Yet they are endangered by habitat loss, climate change, diseases and illegal hunting. We need to work hard to save them.

▶ The money tourists pay to watch mountain gorillas in the wild provides funds for conservation and helps to create jobs for local people.

Index